OPAL DUNN is widely known as a specialist in early first
and second language development. She has been a consultant to
the Council of Europe on children's bilingual education and acts as
consultant to the British Council's LearnEnglish Parents programme.
She has been short-listed for the Eleanor Farjeon award
for services to children's literature and has recently received
the Japanese Rising Sun Award for her contribution to
the international education of Japanese children.
Opal's books for Frances Lincoln are *Acker Backa Boo*,
El Gato Leo Goes to School, *Leo le Chat Goes to School*, *Hippety-hop*, *Hippety-hay*,
Un Deux Trois and *Number Rhymes to Say and Play*.

HANNAH SHAW graduated from Brighton University
with a BA in illustration. Since then she has worked as an illustrator
and author but has also worked in a chocolate shop and as
a visiting lecturer on art courses. She currently lives in a little village
in Gloucestershire with Ben the blacksmith and Ren the dog.
For Frances Lincoln she has also illustrated
Crocodiles Are the Best Animals of All
and *The Grizzly Bear with the Frizzly Hair* by Sean Taylor.

For Nicholas Jasper
O.D.

For Zia
H.S.

BEAN
FOR
SALE

Several of the rhymes have been written by the author to
make understanding of numbers easier for young children.
Any rhyme that is not traditional is derived from its use
in nursery and infant schools with native speaker
or first foreign language learners whom the author
has taught in her long career.
If there is copyright for any of these rhymes, it is an
oversight and the author and publishers will be pleased
to acknowledge it in future editions.

Number Rhymes: Tens and Teens copyright © Frances Lincoln Limited 2009
Text copyright © Opal Dunn 2009
Illustrations copyright © Hannah Shaw 2009
The right of Opal Dunn to be identified as the author and of Hannah Shaw
to be identified as the illustrator of this work has been asserted by them in
accordance with the Copyright, Designs and Patents Act, 1988 (United Kingdom).

First published in Great Britain in 2009 and in the USA in 2010 by
Frances Lincoln Children's Books, 4 Torriano Mews,
Torriano Avenue, London NW5 2RZ
www.franceslincoln.com

First paperback edition published in Great Britain in 2011

A catalogue record for this book is available from the British Library.

ISBN 978-1-84780-230-9

Illustrated with pen and ink and scanned texture
Set in Baskerville

Printed in Heshan, Guangdong, China by Leo Paper Products Ltd. in July 2011
9 8 7 6 5 4 3 2 1

Number Rhymes
Tens and Teens

OPAL DUNN
Illustrated by HANNAH SHAW

F

FRANCES LINCOLN
CHILDREN'S BOOKS

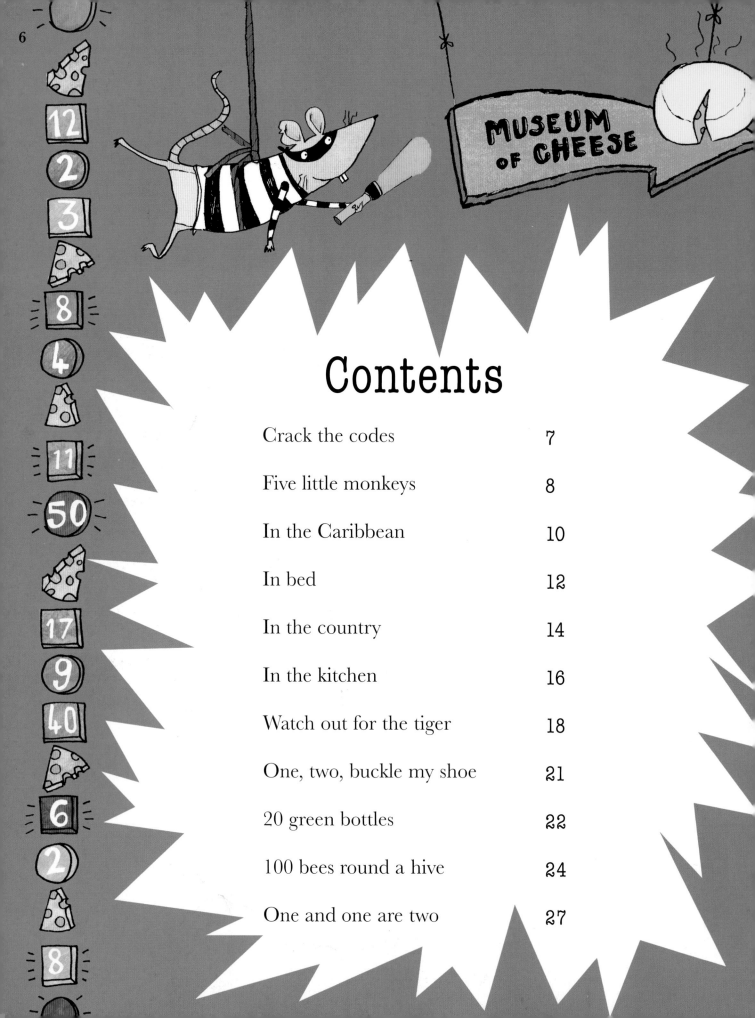

MUSEUM OF CHEESE

Contents

Crack the codes

Listen carefully to the sounds of the numbers bigger than 12.
They are made up in a sort of code. You can easily crack
the code, if you remember these clues:

* Teen means 10
* Thir means 3 so thirteen means 3 and 10
* Fourteen is easy if you remember the code for teen.
* Fif means 5 so fifteen is 5 and 10

Can you work out what numbers make sixteen,
seventeen, eighteen and nineteen? It is quite easy if
you listen to what the words say and remember the
code. You can check the code on pages 22 to 23.

What about twenty? You can crack that code
if you remember this clue:

* Ty means lots of 10
* Twen is 2 so twenty means 2 lots of 10
* Thir is 3 so thirty is 3 lots of 10
* For is 4 so forty is 4 lots of 10

Fifty, sixty, seventy, eighty and ninety
are easy if you listen to what the
words say. You can check the code
on pages 24 to 26.

Numbers are fun! Enjoy the rhymes.

Opal Dunn

8

Five little monkeys

Five little monkeys walked along the shore.
One went a-sailing,
Then there were four.

Four little monkeys climbed up a tree.
One of them tumbled down,
Then there were three.

Three little monkeys found a pot of glue.
One got stuck in it,
Then there were two.

Two little monkeys found a currant bun.
One ran away with it,
Then there was one.

One little monkey cried all afternoon,
So they put him in an aeroplane
And sent him to the moon.

In the Caribbean

One, two, three, four, five, six, seven,
All good children go to heaven;
The clock in heaven strikes eleven,
One, two, three, four, five, six, seven.

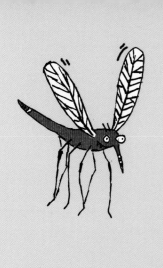

Mosquito one,
Mosquito two,
Mosquito jump in the old man shoe.

Mosquito three,
Mosquito four,
Mosquito open the old man door.

Mosquito five,
Mosquito six,
Mosquito pick up the old man sticks.

Mosquito seven,
Mosquito eight,
Mosquito open the old man gate.

Mosquito nine,
Mosquito ten,
Mosquito bite the old man again.

In bed

There were ten in the bed
And the little one said,
'**Roll over, Roll over**.'
So they all rolled over
And one fell out.

There were nine in the bed
And the little one said,
'**Roll over, Roll over**.'
So they all rolled over
And one fell out.

There were eight in the bed
And the little one said,
'**Roll over, Roll over**.'
So they all rolled over
And one fell out.

There were seven in the bed
And the little one said,
'**Roll over, Roll over**.'
So they all rolled over
And one fell out.

There were six in the bed
And the little one said,
'**Roll over, Roll over**.'
So they all rolled over
And one fell out.

There were five in the bed
And the little one said,
'**Roll over. Roll over**.'
So they all rolled over
And one fell out.

There were four in the bed . . .
There were three in the bed . . .
There were two in the bed . . .
And the little one said,
'**Roll over. Roll over**.'

There was the little one in the bed
And the little one said,
'**I've done it. I've done it**.
I'm the last in the bed!'

In the country

Pigeon and little Wren
Coo, coo, coo!
It's as much as Pigeon can do
To bring up two!

But the little Wren
Can manage ten,
And bring them up
Like gentlemen!

One for the mouse,
One for the crow,
One to rot
And one to grow,
How many did they sow?

Two for the mouse,
Two for the crow,
Two to rot
And two to grow,
How many did they sow?

'Chook, Chook, Chook-chook-chook!'

'Good morning, Mrs Hen.
How many chickens have you got?'

'Madam, I've got ten.
Four of them are yellow,
And four of them are brown,
And two of them are speckled red,
The nicest in the town.'

In the kitchen

Twelve fat sausages sizzling in a pan,
Twelve fat sausages sizzling in a pan.
One went **POP** and the other went **BANG.**
There were ten fat sausages sizzling in the pan.

Ten fat sausages sizzling in a pan,
Ten fat sausages sizzling in a pan.
One went **POP** and the other went **BANG.**
There were eight fat sausages sizzling in the pan.

Eight fat sausages sizzling in a pan,
Eight fat sausages sizzling in a pan.
One went **POP** and the other went **BANG.**
There were six fat sausages sizzling in the pan.

Six fat sausages sizzling in a pan,
Six fat sausages sizzling in a pan.
One went **POP** and the other went **BANG**.
There were four fat sausages sizzling in the pan.

Four fat sausages sizzling in a pan,
Four fat sausages sizzling in a pan.
One went **POP** and the other went **BANG**.
There were two fat sausages sizzling in the pan.

Two fat sausages sizzling in a pan,
Two fat sausages sizzling in a pan.
One went **POP** and the other went **BANG**.
There were no fat sausages sizzling in the pan.

NO fat sausages sizzling in a pan,
NO fat sausages sizzling in a pan.
Nothing went **POP** and nothing went **BANG**.
There were **NO** fat sausages sizzling in the pan.

Watch out for the tiger

MONKEYS
KEEP
OUT

Twelve little monkeys came out to play,
Eating bananas along the way.
Out came a tiger, orange and black,
Eleven little monkeys came running back.

Eleven little monkeys came out to play,
Eating bananas along the way.
Out came a tiger, orange and black,
Ten little monkeys came running back.

Ten little monkeys came out to play,
Eating bananas along the way.
Out came a tiger, orange and black,
Nine little monkeys came running back.

Nine little monkeys came out to play,
Eating bananas along the way.
Out came a tiger, orange and black,
Eight little monkeys came running back.

Eight little monkeys came out to play,
Eating bananas along the way.
Out came a tiger, orange and black,
Seven little monkeys came running back.

Seven little monkeys came out to play,
Eating bananas along the way.
Out came a tiger, orange and black,
Six little monkeys came running back.

Six little monkeys hiding away,
Staying out of the tiger's way.
'**ROAR**,' said the tiger, '**no monkeys here**.'
Look at the monkeys shivering with fear.

One, two, buckle my shoe

1, 2, buckle my shoe

3, 4, knock at the door

5, 6, pick up sticks

7, 8, lay them straight

9, 10, a big fat hen

11, 12, dig and delve

13, 14, maids a-courting

15, 16, maids in the kitchen

17, 18, maids a-waiting

19, 20, my plate's empty

20 green bottles

Twenty green bottles standing on a wall.

Twenty green bottles standing on a wall.

And if two green bottles should accidentally fall,

There'd be eighteen green bottles standing on the wall.

Eighteen green bottles . . .

Sixteen green bottles . . .

Fourteen green bottles . . .

Twelve green bottles . . .

Ten green bottles . . .

Eight green bottles . . .

Six green bottles . . .

Four green bottles . . .

Two green bottles . . .

No green bottles . . .

100 bees round a hive

100 One hundred honey bees
Buzzing round a hive,
Buzz, buzz, buzz,
And ten go inside.

90 Ninety honey bees
Buzzing round a hive,
Buzz, buzz, buzz,
And ten go inside.

80 Eighty honey bees
Buzzing round a hive,
Buzz, buzz, buzz,
And ten go inside.

70 Seventy honey bees
Buzzing round a hive,
Buzz, buzz, buzz,
And ten go inside.

60 Sixty honey bees
Buzzing round a hive,
Buzz, buzz, buzz,
And ten go inside.

50 Fifty honey bees
Buzzing round a hive,
Buzz, buzz, buzz,
And ten go inside.

HONEY BEE CITY

26

40 Forty honey bees
Buzzing round a hive,
Buzz, buzz, buzz,
And ten go inside.

30 Thirty honey bees
Buzzing all the day,
Buzz, buzz, buzz,
And ten go inside.

20 Twenty honey bees.
Buzzing round a hive.
When night comes,
Do they fly away?

One and one are two (1 + 1 = 2)

1 and 1 are 2,
That's for me and you.

2 and 2 are 4,
That's a couple more.

3 and 3 are 6,
Barley-sugar sticks.

4 and 4 are 8,
Tumblers at the gate.

5 and 5 are 10,
Bluff seafaring men.

6 and 6 are 12,
Garden lads to dig and delve.

7 and 7 are 14,
Young men bent on sporting.

8 and 8 are 16,
Pills the doctor's mixing.

9 and 9 are 18,
Passengers kept waiting.

10 and 10 are 20,
Roses pleasant plenty!

2+1=
1+2=3
5+2=6
10+10=
4+4=
11+11 = 22
1+4 =5
1+1=2

11 and 11 are 22,
Sums for brother
George to do.

12 and 12 are 24,
Pretty pictures and no more.

Index of first lines

MORE TITLES BY OPAL DUNN FROM FRANCES LINCOLN CHILDREN'S BOOKS

Number Rhymes to Say and Play
Opal Dunn
Illustrated by Adriano Gon

Here are 18 lively number rhymes and games to help your pre-school child develop and extend numeracy skills. The colourful illustrations reinforce number concepts from 0 to 10 as well as helping to develop language and social skills. By well-known language consultant, Opal Dunn, this book includes practical advice for parents and carers on how to say and play these rhymes. An exciting collection of rhymes guaranteed to have children counting and shouting along.

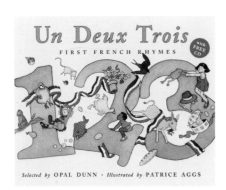

Un Deux Trois
Selected by Opal Dunn
Illustrated by Patrice Aggs

Young children will enjoy learning and speaking French with this collection of simple rhymes and songs, illustrated with a host of characters, animals and birds. A perfect introduction to the sounds and rhythm of another language. With accompanying CD.

Hippety-hop, Hippety-hay
Growing with Rhymes from Birth to Age 3
Opal Dunn
Illustrated by Sally Anne Lambert

Language specialist Opal Dunn has created something very special in this selection of enjoyable, interactive rhymes. Each rhyme has suggested actions and is graded for use according to ages, from babies to three year-olds.